THE DALAI LAMA

A Biography of the
Tibetan Spiritual
and Political Leader

by

DEMI

Henry Holt and Company ⟨ New York

To His Holiness the Dalai Lama

"Better than a thousand useless words
is one single word that gives peace."
— from the *Dhammapada*,
the words of Buddha

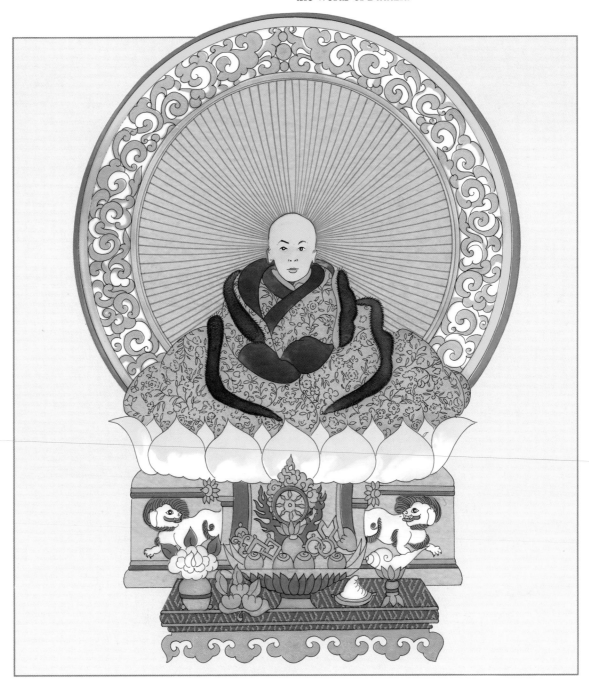

Henry Holt and Company, Inc., *Publishers since 1866,* 115 West 18th Street, New York, New York 10011. Henry Holt is a registered trademark of Henry Holt and Company, Inc. Copyright © 1998 by Demi. All rights reserved. Published in Canada by Fitzhenry & Whiteside Ltd., 195 Allstate Parkway, Markham, Ontario L3R 4T8. Library of Congress Cataloging-in-Publication Data / Demi. The Dalai Lama: a biography of the Tibetan spiritual and political leader / by Demi. 1. Bstan-'dzin-rgya-mtsho, Dalai Lama XIV, 1935- –Juvenile literature. 2. Dalai Lamas–Biography–Juvenile literature. I. Title. BQ7935.B777D46 1998 294.3'923'092–dc21 [B] 97-30654 ISBN 0-8050-5443-X / First Edition–1998. The artist used gouache and ink on vellum and watercolor washes on paper to create the illustrations for this book. Printed in the United States of America on acid-free paper.∞ 10 9 8 7 6 5 4 3 2 1

THE DALAI LAMA

I was born more than sixty years ago in Tibet, a beautiful, open country that lies high in the mountains to the north of India and to the west of China. In this book Demi tells the story of my life since then. I appreciate her effort because my story will also tell you something about the Tibetan people and their unique way of life.

As Dalai Lama, I have a special concern for Tibet and its people. They have placed their trust and hope in me, so I have a responsibility to speak up for them. Therefore, whenever I can, I try to let people know about the real situation inside Tibet.

When I was growing up, Tibetans were free to live as they chose. Many were farmers or looked after large herds of yaks and sheep. Some were merchants travelling here and there to trade, and many, like me, became monks or nuns. They studied large religious books, memorised prayers and learned to train their minds in meditation. In our country, surrounded by snow mountains, with its pure water, clear air and blue skies, we had rich grasslands and thick forests. Even the birds and animals were free from fear, because hunting was not allowed.

Since 1959, Tibet has been occupied by China and many of the things we once loved have been lost. Since 1959 too, I have lived in exile in India with about 100,000 Tibetans who have also left our homeland. Here we have been given help to build new homes, schools and monasteries and to preserve our traditional customs and values. Even though we are refugees, our lives are quite comfortable compared to many of the six million Tibetans whose lives in Tibet are miserable. The dream I am working to fulfil is that one day soon there will be freedom, peace and happiness as there once used to be in Tibet.

July 2, 1997

INTRODUCTION

The land of Tibet is mountainous and magnificent. Its elevation is so high it is known as the "rooftop of the world," and its capital city, Lhasa, is often lit up by heavenly rainbows.

Tibet is one of the most religious countries in the world. Tibetans follow the teachings of Buddha, a holy man born five hundred years before Christ. Every Tibetan village, no matter how small, has its own Buddhist temple, which is the center of Tibetan social religious life.

Buddhists believe in reincarnation, the idea that people are reborn many times on this earth; they believe also that a state of perfection, called Nirvana, can only be achieved after a person has learned many lessons and lived many lives.

Since the 1500s, the Buddhist leader in Tibet has been the Dalai Lama, who is worshiped by people as the bodily form of the Buddhist saint of compassion, Chenrezig. Each new Dalai Lama is believed to be the reincarnation of all the previous ones.

In the Tibetan language, Dalai means "ocean" and Lama means "teacher." So Dalai Lama means "the ocean of wisdom."

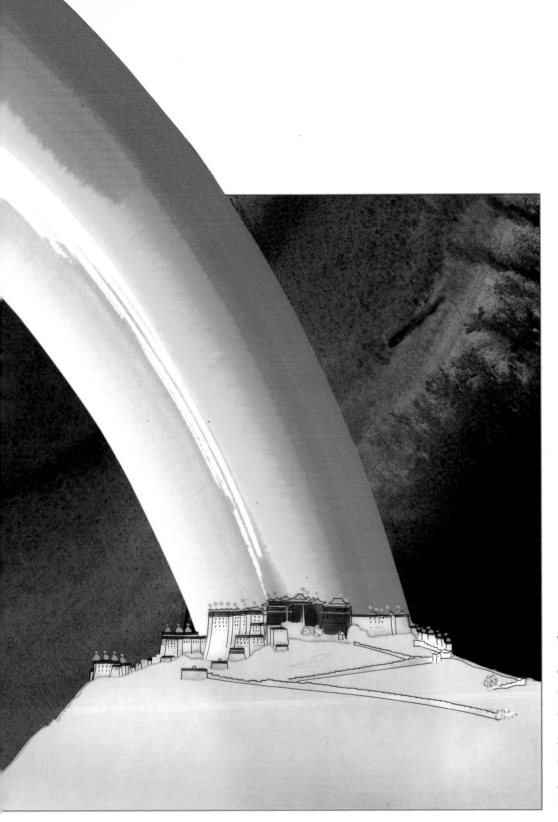

When the thirteenth Dalai Lama died in 1933, the other lamas began the search for the person who would take his place. They believed that his spirit had been reborn in another child. Their task was to find that child and bring him, along with his family, back to the temple in Lhasa.

Lamas began looking for magical signs and omens that would help them find the new Dalai Lama. One lama went up to a sacred lake, Lhamoi Lhatso, high in the mountains, and prayed for guidance. There in the lake the monk saw a vision of a temple with a turquoise roof and a path leading to a small peasant hut. The lama saw three letters,—ཨ *(ah),* ཀ *(ka),* and མ *(ma)*—the first sounds of place names in the east. From this he understood that he should look in the east.

ཨ ཀ མ

Meanwhile, in a small village in eastern Tibet called Takster, a young boy was learning to help with the family chores. His home was very humble but he had two loving parents, an older sister, and three older brothers. The boy liked to churn butter with his mother and weave cloth with his sister. And his brothers let him watch as they sheared the sheep and herded the animals. Best of all, the little boy loved to ride in the fields with his father.

A year passed and the monks still had not found their new spiritual leader. As they got closer to Takster, a beautiful rainbow led them to a small peasant hut and a pathway leading to a temple with a turquoise roof. The hut was the home of the little boy. His name was Lhamo Dhondup.

The monks had heard that Lhamo was a very special child, but they did not yet realize that this was the boy they had been searching for.

People said that when Lhamo was born, his sickly father had become well and the disappointing harvests had become plentiful. They said that as soon as he could speak, he told everyone he was the Dalai Lama and that his real home was in Lhasa. And they said that when he saw the search party, he gathered all his things and declared, "Now I am going home!"

The monks needed to be certain that this was the child they had been looking for, so they began testing him. They believed that if Lhamo were really the Dalai Lama he would be able to remember things from his previous life. So they showed him various objects—things that had belonged to the thirteenth Dalai Lama along with others that had not. Instantly the two-year-old picked out all the correct objects, declaring, "Here is my old walking stick! Here is my ceremonial drum! Here are my prayer beads!"

By then the search party had no doubt that they had found the real fourteenth Dalai Lama.

And so the two-year-old child was taken to Lhasa, accompanied by his extremely happy and proud family. Along the way thousands of Tibetans bowed and prayed to their new infant god-king.

In a grand ceremony on February 22, 1939, when Lhamo was four, he became the fourteenth Dalai Lama and was given the name Getsul Ngawang Lobsang Tenzin Gyatso Sisunwangyal Tsungpa Mapai Dephal Sangpo, which means "the Holy One, the Gentle Glory, Powerful in Speech, Pure in Mind of Divine Wisdom, Holder of the Faith, and Ocean-Wide." But until he was fifteen, a regent was to rule the country in his place.

At the age of five, the Dalai Lama began his training with the high lamas in the enormous Potala Palace. He had two tutors. They taught him math, science, history, and languages. They also taught him passages from Buddhist holy books. From these books, called sutras, the little Dalai Lama learned about the kindness and compassion that bring wisdom.

His only playmates were one of his older brothers and the mice. In his huge, cold bedroom at night, the little Dalai Lama would watch the mice running up and down his curtains.

The Dalai Lama was bright, curious, mischievous, and, to his teachers, a "holy terror." He was fascinated with mechanical things. He took apart all the clocks in the palace, then put them back together again. The lamas were forbidden to punish the Dalai Lama, so they punished his brother instead. As the little Dalai Lama loved his brother so very much, he tried not to be too mischievous.

At the age of seven, the Dalai Lama discovered a telescope. He used it to look at all the children of Lhasa playing in the streets. He also found an old movie projector and got it running.

When the Dalai Lama got older, he repaired a 1927 Austin-Healey. He began driving around the palace and smashed into a tree in the courtyard. Afterward, he fixed its broken headlights by cutting new pieces of glass and smearing them with syrup to make them look as old as before.

At the age of thirteen, the Dalai Lama began studying serious subjects such as philosophy, calligraphy, and metaphysics. He memorized whole passages from Buddhist books and joined in debates where the lamas actually danced out the finer points of Buddhism. He soon became an expert.

In 1950, when he was fifteen, the Dalai Lama was named the spiritual and political leader of Tibet. But as the Dalai Lama read in the peace and quiet of the palace, war was brewing outside.

In 1950, the Communist Chinese imposed control over Tibet, causing great hardships to the Tibetan people. Buddhism was repressed. The countryside was devastated and the economy bankrupted. Tibet was in chaos.

In 1954, at the age of nineteen, the Dalai Lama went to Beijing, the capital of China, to make peace with Chairman Mao Tse-tung, the Communist leader, but peace was not to be made.

The Communist Cultural Revolution swept across the Chinese continent, which resulted in massive destruction and human suffering. Uncounted numbers of national treasures, holy books, and temples were burned and ruined. Tibet was not spared from this madness.

In 1959, the Communist Chinese army invaded Tibet. Hundreds of Buddhist monasteries were destroyed and thousands of monks arrested or killed. On the night of March 17, the Dalai Lama and a small party began a harrowing two-week escape from Tibet to India. Disguised as an ordinary person, the Dalai Lama managed to elude the soldiers of the Communist army. But after many days of no sleep, bad food, and

the thin air of the highest mountain passes, the Dalai Lama became ill. He had to be strapped to the back of a yak for the rest of the journey into India. Finally, on March 31, the Dalai Lama emerged from the woods. He was twenty-four and his life in exile had begun.

Thousands of Tibetans soon followed their spiritual leader to India. In Dharamsala, he formed a government-in-exile. He set up centers to preserve Tibetan art, holy scriptures, and medicine. He organized free public schools where Tibetan was spoken. All of this served—and still serves—as a model for a restored Tibet.

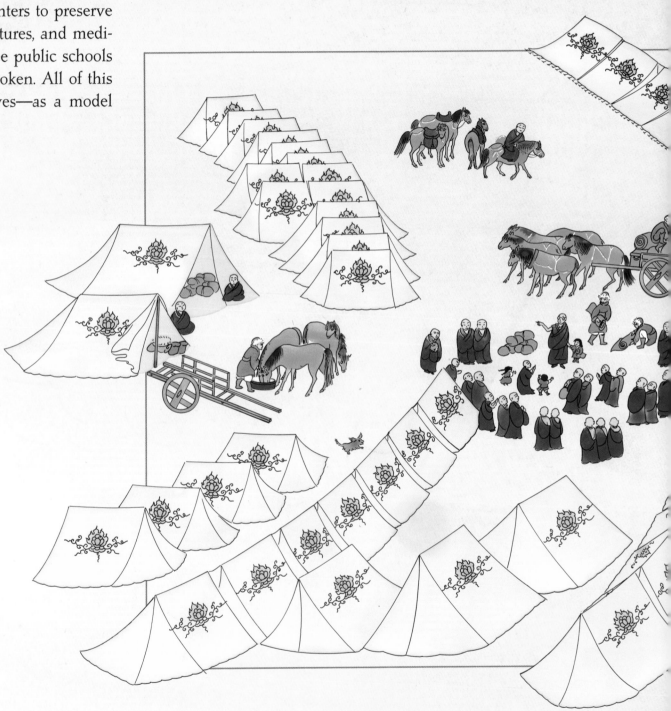

The Dalai Lama continues to live the spiritual life of a monk. He listens to the sad stories of those who have fled from Tibet. "My true religion," he says, "is kindness. There is not one waking hour when I don't think of the plight of my people."

Today, the Dalai Lama travels the world, giving speeches that have brought international attention to the plight of Tibet. He speaks of peace and compassion. He reminds his listeners that there has never been a war fought in the name of Buddha, and that war is not stopped by war but by peace and love.

In 1989, the Dalai Lama received the Nobel Peace Prize. At the ceremony, he said, "Because we all share this small planet earth, we have to learn to live in harmony and peace with each other and with nature.

"Live simply and love humanity. For as long as space endures and for as long as living beings remain, until then may I, too, abide to dispel the misery of the world."

The Dalai Lama's work for peace continues to this day.